Arnold Schwarzenegger

Arnold Schwarzenegger

by Jack North

 **DILLON PRESS**
New York

Maxwell Macmillan Canada
Toronto

Maxwell Macmillan International
New York   Oxford   Singapore   Sydney

Photo Credits

Front Cover: Retna Pictures, Ltd. (Arnal/Garcia/Stills)
Back Cover: AP—Wide World Photos

Retna Pictures, Ltd.: P/A/G (2, 57); Dave Allocca (5, 28); Steve Granitz (10, 16, 19, 22, 30, 38, 53, 55); Rocky Widner (12, 21); Koch (33); Frederic Garcia (35); Sabat (48); Bill Davila (60)
AP—Wide World Photos: 6, 8, 20, 24, 42, 44, 46, 58

Book design by Carol Matsuyama

Library of Congress Cataloging-in-Publication Data

North, Jack.
   Arnold Schwarzenegger / by Jack North.
     p. cm. — (Taking part)
     ISBN 0-87518-638-6   0-382-24726-4 (pbk.)
     1. Schwarzenegger, Arnold—Juvenile literature. 2. Bodybuilders—United States—Biography—Juvenile literature. 3. Motion picture actors and actresses—United States—Biography—Juvenile literature. I. Title. II. series.
   GV545.52.S38N67   1994
   646.7'5'092—dc20
   [B]   93-40891

Summary: A biography of the Austrian bodybuilder whose action-adventure movies have made him one of the biggest stars in Hollywood.

Dillon Press   Maxwell Macmillan Canada, Inc.
Macmillan Publishing Company   1200 Eglinton Avenue East
866 Third Avenue   Suite 200
New York, NY 10022   Don Mills, Ontario M3C 3N1

Macmillan Publishing Company is part of the Maxwell Communications Group of Companies.

First Edition

Printed in the United States of America

10 9 8 7 6 5 4 3 2 1

Contents

1

"Ar-nold! Ar-nold!"

From miles away you see the beams of light shooting into the clouds. You follow the lights to their source—a movie theater surrounded by a crowd of cheering fans. A film is premiering here tonight, and although you need an invitation to get inside, everyone is free to stand along the velvet ropes and stargaze.

Limousines are pulling up to the roped-off area, dropping off celebrities at the end of the red carpet. Fans "ooh" and "ah" at the array of famous guests. But you're waiting for the brightest star, the name that fills the brightly lit theater marquee . . .

SCHWARZENEGGER

The next car is not a limousine, but a loud, over-sized Jeep, which the army calls a Humvee. Who else would drive such an outrageous, macho vehicle?

He's all muscle. He's a bodybuilding legend. He's

Enjoying his status as one of the most popular stars in Hollywood, Arnold kisses his People's Choice Award for favorite movie actor.

Arnold and his wife, reporter Maria Shriver, kneel beside his star on Hollywood's Walk of Fame.

one of the highest-paid performers in the world. He's the actor who can send thrills, chills, and laughter rippling through an audience.

"Ar-nold! Ar-nold!" The crowd begins to chant his name as he bolts out of the car.

His face and hulking physique are unmistakable. Who could imitate that steely jaw? That cocky, curled lip? That massive body, dubbed the Austrian Oak?

He waves, and the crowd goes wild, cheering, chanting, and whooping with excitement. Few fans have ever come so close to a star of this magnitude.

In the film industry, Arnold Schwarzenegger is a powerhouse, a "bankable" star who lures audiences to see a film just because he appears in it. How did a young boy from Austria become an international celebrity?

Arnold's success is no accident. It came with hard work, planning, determination, courage . . . and a lively sense of humor that is exclusively Arnold's.

2

The Kid from Thal

Picture a small Austrian village surrounded by rolling hills, lakes, and lush green forests. In the distance, you can see the snow-capped Alps. Horses graze in the nearby meadows. And if you take a stroll on a summer afternoon, you'll find fields laced with yellow buttercups and hedges of sweet-smelling lilacs.

That's the village of Thal, where Arnold spent his childhood. It may sound more like a country retreat than the birthplace of a superstar, but the town proved to be the perfect training ground for a young boy who was not always the biggest, the strongest, or the toughest.

Born July 30, 1947, Arnold was the second son of Gustav and Aurelia Schwarzenegger. Their first son, Meinhard, had been born the previous summer.

Although Arnold is said to have inherited his physique from his grandfather Karl, a big, strapping

Arnold has come a long way from the little town in Austria where he grew up.

Arnold wasn't always a muscleman. As a boy, he was small and quiet.

steelworker, Arnold's infancy was fraught with illness. Since there was no doctor in Thal, his parents often had to carry him into Graz, the nearest town with medical care. Graz was only four miles away from Thal, but the Schwarzeneggers did not own horses or a car, which meant the trip was made on foot.

Even after his health was restored, young Arnold was hardly a miniature man of steel. Some people remember him as a shy kid with thick glasses and ears that stuck out. But despite his quiet manner, Arnold took an interest in the world around him.

One of his classmates, Helga Verschink, remembers Arnold as a boy who defended the underdog. "Arnold always protected me because I was small," she told one journalist.

From an early age, Arnold had a strong sense of heroic justice, and he was blessed with parents who encouraged him to be the best.

Arnold's father was chief of police and played in the local police officers's band. A tall, handsome man, Gustav Schwarzenegger was a talented musician, able to play six different instruments. He loved to amuse and entertain, a quality that seems to have been passed on to his second son.

Gustav encouraged his sons to explore the world around them. For Arnold's father, education meant more than sitting in the classroom at Hans Gross School, which Arnold began attending at the age of six. Arnold's father pushed his sons to be active, outgoing, and inquisitive.

Young Arnold and Meinhard spent weekends discovering the inner workings of country farms. They went hiking in the hills. When the police band was performing, they went to watch their father. And sometimes they went into Graz to attend plays and visit art museums.

However, at the end of each weekend, their father made the boys write essays describing how they'd spent their weekend. A firm believer in education, Gustav even graded the papers! The boys dreaded those essays. But those early challenges may have given Arnold the confidence to tackle bigger feats in his adult life.

Arnold's mother, Aurelia, was a meticulously neat

brunette who worked hard to keep her family healthy and comfortable. It was no easy task in a 300-year-old house with no heating and no indoor plumbing. Whenever it was time to clean house or wash clothes, she had to fetch water from a pump behind the house and tote it up the stairs. Whether she was down on her hands and knees scrubbing the cold wooden floors or kneading dough for homemade strudel, Arnold's mother went about her chores with a firm resolve.

In a time when many Europeans had to work hard just to feed their children, the Schwarzenegger family was also struggling.

"There was no food around," Arnold recalls. He remembers chewing on orange peels that he got from other kids. He didn't get to taste his first banana until he was eleven. Meat was a luxury, though Arnold's mother tried to serve it once a week—usually Wiener schnitzel for Sunday dinner.

Food wasn't the only thing that was scarce in the Schwarzenegger home. There was no television. The family couldn't afford a refrigerator until Arnold was older, and Arnold remembers the day when it finally

Arnold flexes for the camera.

arrived. The whole family kept sticking their hands into the cool, frosty box with looks of amazement.

"It was a rough upbringing," Arnold recalls. But he believes that those years spent doing without treats, toys, and new clothes helped make him the success he is today. Those days of personal sacrifice inspired an ambition in Arnold. "When something is missing— that's what creates this drive," he explains.

And although Gustav and Aurelia could not give their son all the material things he desired, they provided the things that truly mattered. "My parents gave me confidence," says Arnold. "They supported me and gave me their love."

Another source of support and camaraderie throughout Arnold's childhood was his older brother. Meinhard was a playmate, competitor, and coconspirator for Arnold, and the two boys shared a strong brotherly bond.

It was Meinhard who exposed Arnold to his first taste of Hollywood glitz—when Arnold was only six years old! Meinhard brought his brother into town to see a visiting American celebrity, a man named Johnny Weissmuller. At the time, Weissmuller was a famed Olympic swimmer and actor. His athletic skills had won him the role of Tarzan in the popular films about the strong, courageous jungle hero.

The sight of a flesh-and-blood Hollywood hero

seemed to have made an impression on Arnold. Although the six-year-old couldn't have known what the future held for him, his love of screen heroes was born.

At home, the two boys shared a bedroom. From their window, they could see the ruins of an ancient castle. Who knows what dreams filled the boys' heads as they slept near the tumbled castle walls? Perhaps there were thoughts of knighthood, ancient battles that had been fought . . . or maybe even the first musings of the hero from prehistoric times—Conan the Barbarian—a role Arnold would portray on screen in his adult years.

In a way, Arnold was the underdog at home. Often pitted against his older brother in boxing matches or ski competitions, Arnold rose to the challenge. "Let's see who's the best!" cried their father, and the two boys raced or ran or boxed with all their might.

Fortunately, the landscape of southern Austria had much to offer a pair of active boys. In the winter months there was skiing and ice-skating on the frozen Thalersee, a nearby lake. In the summer the boys

Arnold goes out on the town with his mom and his wife.

played tennis and went hiking in the woods. They went swimming or boating on the lake, which was filled with ducks and lined with shady trees in the warm months. Before he reached his teens, Arnold went out for team sports in Graz, where he played a wing position on a local soccer team.

With the rolling hills of Austria as a childhood playground, it's no wonder that Arnold started his public career as a bodybuilder. His love of exercise emerged in

Arnold encourages a group of young Special Olympics athletes during their workout.

his childhood, and it's still a key element in his current physical fitness crusade.

At the age of 13, Arnold discovered another world that was very different from the Austrian village he called home. For just six schillings, he could walk through the door of a movie theater and get an eyeful of amazing feats and spectacles on film.

Arnold was captivated.

The year was 1960, and epic films like *Spartacus* and *Ben-Hur* were making the run at theaters. But at the time, Arnold wasn't interested in seeing Academy Award winners or art films. "Who wants to see people talk and have a good time?" Arnold says when asked

An avid sportsman since childhood, Arnold takes a run down a snowy slope.

Arnold with two other action movie superstars—Sylvester Stallone and Bruce Willis.

about his teenage taste in films. "I wanted to see violence and hanky-panky."

On the silver screen, action and adventure were easy to find—along with a whole posse of rough-and-tough heroes.

There was John Wayne, one of the coolest cowboys

to walk away from a smoking gun.

There was Johnny Weissmuller as Tarzan, the agile, courageous man who understood the ways of the rain forest.

And there was Reg Park, an actor who brought to life the role of Hercules, a mythological hero noted for his incredible strength.

Arnold saw *Hercules* many times. He studied the actor's moves and stunts. He heard the same lines over and over. He thrilled to the battle scenes countless times. And he promised himself that one day he would be a superhero like Hercules.

In a dark cinema in Graz, Arnold began to set his sights on stardom. On the other side of the world, in Hollywood, California, people made careers starring in motion picture films. Even as a kid, Arnold knew one thing for sure: "I wanted to be part of that action."

3

Pumping Iron

When he was 13, Arnold Schwarzenegger began the pursuit that would bring him worldwide fame—body-building.

For inspiration, he had the example of one famous bodybuilder who had become a star. Reg Park, the man who played the heroic Hercules on the silver screen, was also a bodybuilder. If pumping iron would produce muscles like those of the mighty Hercules, then working out was the first step Arnold would take.

Unlike other kids who watched movie heroes with admiration, Arnold made the decision to match their achievements—no matter how much work, sweat, and sacrifice it took.

"As a kid I always idolized the winning athletes," Arnold told one journalist. "It is one thing to idolize heroes. It is quite another to visualize yourself in their place. When I saw great people, I said to myself: 'I can be there.'"

Arnold shows off the pumped-up body that won him the title of Mr. Universe.

25

Arnold Schwarzenegger

Aware that he had much to learn about this sport, Arnold talked his way into a gymnasium where bodybuilders worked out. He asked around until he found someone who knew a local bodybuilder named Kurt Marnul, who won the title of Mr. Austria in the 1960s. When Arnold heard that the swimming master at the Thalersee was friends with Marnul, he pestered the man until he had no choice but to ask the bodybuilder to meet with Arnold, his biggest fan.

Fortunately for Arnold, Kurt Marnul agreed to the meeting. One summer day, he came to Arnold's village for a swim in the Thalersee, where he met his teenage fan. Impressed by Arnold's ambition, Marnul invited him to come and work out in the Athletic Union Graz, a gym that Marnul had founded in 1958.

Arnold didn't waste a minute. The next day, when Marnul arrived at the gym, Arnold was waiting on the doorstep.

It was hardly a luxurious gym. There was no carpeting on the floor. There was no heat. The wall had a hole in it, which the athletes plugged up with old newspapers. On windy nights, the papers would fly out, letting in the chilly winter air.

But Arnold ignored the primitive conditions. He had come to the Union to train. And from the very first training session, he began to learn from watching the other two dozen bodybuilders who worked out there.

Kurt Marnul gave Arnold basic training advice and encouraged the young athlete to push himself to the limit. Marnul also instructed Arnold on diet, telling him to consume foods that were high in protein, such as eggs and meat. Although Arnold would have liked to follow the older man's diet to the letter, his parents still could not afford to feed their children meat every day.

Soon, Arnold's life was spent traveling from Thal, where he was still living with his parents and attending school, to Graz, where he trained. At five o'clock each evening when the gym opened, Arnold was waiting at the door. And at night, he sometimes missed the bus because he wanted to stay and finish off his last set. When that happened, Arnold had to walk the four miles back to Thal.

It was a grueling schedule for a teenage boy, but Arnold was totally dedicated. Karl Kainrath, a body-

Arnold works out with the son of boxing great Evander Holyfield.

builder who worked out with Arnold at the Union, recalls Arnold's determination. "We all knew that the building could have fallen down," said Kainrath, "but Arnold would still have continued training."

As Arnold became as familiar as a barbell at the gym, the other athletes got a taste of his sense of humor. Arnold liked to joke with the other bodybuilders. Sometimes he made them laugh so hard they had to stop their training.

Arnold also gained a reputation as a master of practical jokes. While he was training in Graz, another young bodybuilder asked Arnold the secret to his success. Was it his diet?

According to the story, Arnold told the hopeful athlete that he needed to add salt and ground nutshells to his diet. The diet began with a spoonful of salt and nutshells the first day. The dose should be increased to two spoonfuls the second day, three the third, and so on . . . until thirty spoonfuls were consumed on the thirtieth day.

Of course, Arnold was just kidding! Large doses of salt are not at all healthy. And salt is especially bad for bodybuilders because it makes the body retain liquid.

But apparently the young athlete believed Arnold and started the diet immediately. The athlete stopped the diet when it produced some ill effects. But the guys at the gym who knew about Arnold's prank enjoyed a few laughs over the practical joke.

When Arnold was just 15 years old, he began a three-year apprenticeship with a construction firm in Graz. He earned a good salary working as a carpenter, but most important, the job gave him the money and the freedom to keep training.

Arnold jokes around with Sylvester the Cat.

By that time, Arnold was working out every day. When the Union was closed on Saturday and Sunday, he trained on his own. Sometimes he used the makeshift gym set up in his parents' basement. Other times he trained with his friend Karl Gerstl, another teenager who kept weights and other equipment in his parents' large apartment in Graz.

Arnold was still in his midteens when he entered his first bodybuilding contest. The event was held in the Steirer Hof, a fancy hotel in Graz. Although Arnold did not win the contest, he was a runner-up. And the contest served as a good introduction for Arnold, who warmed to the audience's applause whenever he flexed his newly developed muscles.

Encouraged by the thrill of competition, Arnold set his sights on other contests. In order to compete on a large scale, he knew he would have to leave Austria. But before Arnold had a chance to enter his second competition, his career turned in a different direction.

In the beginning of October 1965, Arnold began his mandatory one-year stint with the Austrian Army. He had just turned 18.

Arnold Schwarzenegger

For the most part, military service offered a lifestyle that Arnold enjoyed. Thanks to the army canteen, Arnold got to eat meat every day for the first time in his life. His body responded to the plentiful supply of protein, which added to his muscular bulk.

As a tank driver, Arnold had a chance to experience the thrill of controlling the massive machines and their big guns. In his autobiography, *Arnold: The Education of a Bodybuilder*, Arnold describes the excitement of operating tanks and the powerful weapons. He loved the recoil of the guns. The sheer strength of each explosion was unmatched by anything he'd ever witnessed.

Still, life in the army was not without its pitfalls. On one occasion, Arnold forgot to set the brake on a tank, and the supposedly parked vehicle rolled into the river!

And Arnold's military commitment posed a problem in his first month of service. He'd been invited to Stuttgart, Germany, to compete in the Junior Mr. Europe Contest on October 30. Arnold couldn't bear to miss the contest. But the army wouldn't allow him the time off.

Arnold decided to disobey his military orders and go

Arnold was so dedicated to his career as a bodybuilder that he once deserted his army post without permission, to compete in a contest.

AWOL (absent without leave). He knew he would be punished when he returned to the army camp in Graz. But in the meantime, Arnold could not resist the chance to advance his bodybuilding career.

At the Stuttgart event, Arnold made a huge splash. He won the contest and became Junior Mr. Europe 1965. He also met people who would play major roles in his future.

Also competing was Franco Columbu, a bodybuilder who would become a good friend of Arnold's. Years later, Franco would be included in Arnold's wedding party. The two men are still good friends today.

Two men in the audience also befriended Arnold. One was Wag Bennett, a British bodybuilder and promoter who owned a gym in London. The other was Rolf Putziger, owner of a gym in Munich, Germany. He offered Arnold a job managing his gym, a position that Arnold accepted the following year.

After the competition, Arnold had to face the music back in the army. He remembers spending seven days locked in the military jail. During that week he was given very little food. He had to sleep on a cold stone bench with only one blanket to keep warm. But the glory of his Junior Mr. Europe title was worth the sacrifice.

Six months later, Arnold won his second major bodybuilding title—Mr. Germany. He was on a roll. Unfortunately, his parents did not think bodybuilding was a suitable career. After his release from the army, they wanted him to settle down in Thal and work as a carpenter in Graz. It would have been a safe, secure life

Throughout his career, Arnold has attributed his success to a positive outlook and a determination to succeed.

Arnold Schwarzenegger

for Arnold. But he wanted more, and he was willing to take some risks to follow his dreams.

"Good things don't happen by coincidence," Arnold told one reporter. "Every dream carries with it certain risks."

Not one to take the safe route, Arnold packed his bags and moved to Munich at the age of 19. Working as the manager of Putziger's gym, he did not earn a huge salary. When he first arrived in town without savings, he slept on the gym floor. But the job at the gym gave Arnold the chance to pump iron. He trained every day, sometimes for as long as seven hours.

His strict training regimen brought great results.

In September 1966, two months after he'd started working in Munich, Arnold flew to London for the Mr. Universe contest. Sponsored by the National Amateur Body Builders Association (NABBA), the contest was a major event for bodybuilders.

Arnold came in second that year. But the crowd was awed by the newcomer—the Austrian Oak.

No one was surprised the following year when Arnold won the 1967 Mr. Universe title. Weighing in at

235 pounds, 6-foot 2-inch Arnold Schwarzenegger was no longer a shy boy with ears that stuck out. His arms measured 22 inches. His thighs were 28 1/2 inches. And his chest was a broad 57 inches! Just 20 years old, Arnold was the youngest Mr. Universe in the history of the contest!

By this time, one of the most famous bodybuilders in all of Europe, Arnold was invited to spend the Christmas holidays with his idol, Reg Park! Arnold was flown to South Africa, where he spent the holiday with Reg and his wife, Marianne.

Twenty-year-old Arnold was overwhelmed by Reg's fancy home. The place was filled with priceless antiques and many servants. Young Arnold was unaccustomed to such a lavish lifestyle. At the time, he couldn't have known that his own wealth and fame would one day eclipse the career of a man like Park.

Arnold was voted Mr. Universe a second time in 1968. The Austrian Oak now dominated bodybuilding contests throughout Europe.

His next challenge was a new competition on another continent—North America.

4

Living in the U.S.A.

When Arnold arrived in the United States in 1968, he went through the customs line in Miami, Florida, with just one gym bag. Having come to compete in a contest, he didn't plan to stay long. But his short stay would eventually stretch into a new life.

"I could not speak the language well at all," Arnold recalls. "It was the most difficult time in my life."

Arnold had been flown to the States at the expense of a bodybuilding promoter named Joe Weider. A former bodybuilder himself, Weider dedicated his career to promoting and improving the sport. Along with his brother, Ben, Joe published magazines that focused on bodybuilding. The Weiders also founded the International Federation of Body Builders (IFBB), an association that sponsored its own Mr. Universe contest.

It was this IFBB event that had brought Arnold to

Arnold chats with actor and director Clint Eastwood at a movie premier.

Arnold Schwarzenegger

Miami at the age of 21. With just one day to recover from jet lag, Arnold appeared at the Miami Beach Auditorium and struck his most impressive poses to the strains of the song "Exodus." But despite his success in Europe, Arnold lost to the bodybuilder Frank Zane.

Alone in a strange country, Arnold could have been shattered by the loss. But after the initial disappointment, Arnold says that the defeat only spurred his determination. His inner strength pulled him through. "Strength does not come from winning," Arnold had once said. "Your struggles develop your strengths. When you go through hardships and decide not to surrender, that is strength."

Arnold was not about to surrender.

Likewise, promoter Joe Weider refused to give up on the young European. Years later, Weider told a journalist, "There was absolutely no question that Arnold was a sleeping giant just waiting to be roused to reach the greatness he was slated for." Although it would take some time to wake the giant, once Arnold sprang to the top of America's bodybuilding world, there would be no stopping him.

During Arnold's first few years in the United States, Weider lent his support. Weider paid Arnold a salary and provided him with a car and an apartment in the beachside community of Santa Monica, California. In turn, Arnold helped to sell Weider's magazines and a positive image of bodybuilding.

The warm sunshine of southern California agreed with Arnold. He could go to the gym for a morning workout, spend the afternoon tanning at the beach, then return to the gym for another set of repetitions in the evening.

Although Arnold fell in with a group of bodybuilders who trained together at Gold's Gym in Santa Monica, he also convinced Weider to hire his old friend Franco Columbu. The two men moved into a two-bedroom apartment on 14th Street in Santa Monica. According to local legend, Arnold and Franco set up a bricklaying business called Pumping Bricks. Some say the business was just a gimmick to get publicity for bodybuilding. But during their appearances on TV talk shows, the two men told some amusing stories about things that had gone wrong while "pumping bricks."

*Former President George Bush presents Arnold with an award
for his work with the Special Olympics.*

42

In 1969, Arnold suffered another American defeat. He lost both the IFBB Mr. Universe and the Mr. Olympia to Sergio Oliva. Although Arnold did win the NABBA Mr. Universe contest in London that year, he decided it was time to revamp his training method. He gave up his long daily sessions. Instead, he used Joe Weider's technique, training with one-hour sessions two or three times a day.

Finally, in 1970, Arnold's new training regime paid off. In London, he won the 1970 NABBA Mr. Universe contest. The next day, having spent much of the time jetting across the globe, Arnold appeared in Columbus, Ohio, to compete in the Pro Mr. World contest. He won in Columbus, then won again two weeks later at the Mr. Olympia contest in New York City.

It seemed that 1970 was Arnold's year for victory. But the winning had just begun. Arnold went on to win the Mr. Olympia title for the next five years. When the 1975 contest was held in Pretoria, South Africa, the event ended with a surprise announcement.

The stage was lit for cameras, which were recording the 1975 contest for a documentary film called

Arnold in a publicity shot for Pumping Iron

Pumping Iron. As the cameras rolled, Arnold defeated Lou Ferrigno, the bodybuilder who played on the television show *The Incredible Hulk*. Then Arnold beat his friend Franco Columbu.

After Arnold was handed the trophy by his old friend and idol Reg Park, he turned to the cameras and announced that he would no longer compete. He acknowledged that the sport had been a great experience for him. And he vowed that he would never stop bodybuilding.

Much to the surprise of the athletes and fans who surrounded him, Arnold Schwarzenegger was retiring from bodybuilding competition when he was 28.

Of course, Arnold remained close to the sport that had brought him fame. He had spent a lot of time and energy promoting bodybuilding.

When he had begun pumping iron in his teens, the sport was not always taken seriously. Critics claimed that it was just a beauty contest. They didn't see the point of athletes getting up on stage and posing. Other people accused bodybuilders of being narcissistic—in love with themselves.

But Arnold had changed many of those negative perceptions. He had brought fame, respect, and attention to the sport. Even after he left competition, his commitment to the sport lived on.

He produced the 1976 Mr. Olympia contest in Columbus, Ohio. As a sports commentator, he covered some of the bodybuilding events for television broadcast. He worked to raise cash prizes for bodybuilding contests. His own competition, the Arnold Cup, has offered prize money in the range of $150,000.

Arnold poses for an audience at the opening of Pumping Iron *in France.*

And in 1980, Arnold surprised the bodybuilding world by returning to competition one last time, at the Mr. Olympia contest in Sydney, Australia. Arnold won the title, making him a seven-time winner of the Mr. Olympia crown.

Arnold Schwarzenegger became the undisputed king of the bodybuilding world. But even before he announced his retirement, he had begun working on a second career—in a medium that would make him bigger than life and bring him megastardom. Enter Arnold the actor.

5

"I'll Be Back!"

Arnold was still a bodybuilding contender when he appeared in his first film, *Hercules Goes Bananas* (sometimes called *Hercules in New York*). Shot in 1969, the low-budget film was made for Italian television. Arnold appeared under the pseudonym "Arnold Strong." Although the film cannot be counted among one of Arnold's triumphs, it was a learning experience for him.

In 1975, Arnold flew to Alabama to begin filming *Stay Hungry* with Sally Field and Jeff Bridges. This time, Arnold worked with acting coach Eric Morris, who praised Arnold's talents. "He is one of the smartest people I have ever met," says Morris. "Very few people realize how talented he really is." When the film opened, Arnold was nominated for a Hollywood Golden Globe award as most promising newcomer.

While *Stay Hungry* brought Arnold his first expo-

A caricature depicts Arnold as his most famous character, the Terminator.

Arnold Schwarzenegger

sure to experienced actors, *Conan the Barbarian* brought him his first big financial success on the screen. But when the movie was filmed in Spain, it was hardly a glamorous venture. First they shot in Segovia, where Arnold endured subzero temperatures. Then the crew moved to another location, where they had to deal with blistering heat and swarming mosquitoes.

Through it all, Arnold emerged as a hero on and off the screen. He learned sword fighting and did all his own stunts, which did not always go right. "In the first scene I had to be attacked by four live wolves," Arnold recalled. But the crew let the wolves out of the cage too quickly. Arnold ran backward and cut his back on the rocks. He needed stitches before filming could go on.

The success of Arnold's Conan prompted a sequel, *Conan the Destroyer*, which was released in 1984. Although the film scored at the box office, it was eclipsed by a surprise hit released later that year, a film called *The Terminator*.

In what some people say was one of Arnold's greatest films, he played a cyborg robot, the ultimate villain. Arnold enjoyed working with the futuristic vehicles and weird weapons used in the film. He created a fashion trend with his black leather jacket and reflective sunglasses. And no one can forget his trademark Terminator line: "I'll be back."

Clearly a hit as an adventure hero, Arnold starred in a number of action films, including *Commando, Predator, Red Heat,* and *Total Recall.*

The filming of *Red Heat* took Arnold back to Europe, and one location was close to his old stomping grounds in Graz. Arnold was happy to be near his childhood home, which he had visited often since his departure in 1968, and his mother, Aurelia, visited the set a few times. But the shooting of *Red Heat* also brought tragedy when Benny Dobbins, Arnold's stuntman, died of a sudden heart attack. According to one report, Arnold was very upset by the loss of his coworker and friend.

In 1986, Arnold took on a new roll—offscreen— that brought him a great deal of publicity. On a cool April day in Hyannis, Massachusetts, he married Maria Shriver. His bride, the dark-haired TV journalist and niece of former President John F. Kennedy, has been likened to the closest thing to a princess America could offer.

Their match has spurred a flurry of political jokes, since the Kennedys are a Democratic family and Arnold is a staunch Republican. However, despite their political conflicts, Arnold enjoys Maria's company immensely. Said Arnold, "Whether we're traveling or horseback riding or going to art galleries or hanging out with her family or my mother, we love to be together."

Marriage didn't seem to change the busy lifestyle of either Arnold or Maria. After their honeymoon in Antigua, Arnold returned to California to pursue his film projects, while Maria went back to her CBS news beat in New York. However, some friends speculated that marriage was changing Arnold. "The people around me say that I have become kinder since I got married," Arnold told one reporter. "That I am more low-key, more considerate, and more the homebody."

Was the world about to see a kinder, gentler Arnold?

Although he did not seem to make any drastic changes, his marriage may have been one of the events

Arnold and Maria arrive at the premier of Twins.

that prompted Arnold to take on some different film roles—beginning with his part in 1988's *Twins*. Turning from action to comedy, Arnold played the un-identical twin brother of Danny DeVito.

Ivan Reitman, the director of *Twins*, was impressed by Arnold's bigger-than-life quality. "Certain people just jump off the screen, and there's no way to explain it," said Reitman. But *Twins* also revealed Arnold's warm, vulnerable qualities. When the film opened, Reitman went up to Maria Shriver and told her, "People will finally understand why you married Arnold." He was right. The film was a hit, as was Arnold's humorous portrayal of a "gentle giant."

Arnold Schwarzenegger

Arnold enjoyed his role in *Twins*. "I feel more comfortable with gentle scenes than violent ones," he said. But he also remembers the filming of one scene that made him a little uneasy. He had to sing on an airplane, and Arnold does not pride himself on his ability to carry a tune. "There were a hundred people, and I was there to sing," he said. "*That's* embarrassing. But as soon as I do it and people laugh, then I know it will work on the screen the same way. So it becomes, then, a plus."

In 1990, Arnold worked with Ivan Reitman again on *Kindergarten Cop*, a lighthearted film that placed Arnold in a classroom of five-year-olds. He rose—or dropped—to the occasion, getting down on his knees so that he could be eye-to-eye with his young costars.

The kinder, gentler Arnold was even apparent in the reprisal of his famous role, for *Terminator 2: Judgment Day*. Although Arnold played the tough, steely cyborg from the future, this time he was a good, fatherly robot who'd come not to kill the boy but to save him.

T2 blew audiences out of their seats, taking in more than $200 million in the United States alone. People

Arnold and his Twins *costar, Danny DeVito*

Arnold Schwarzenegger

loved the dynamite special effects. Critics agreed that the story was as well crafted as the original *Terminator*. And fans thrilled to Arnold's new role as iron-man savior of the world. True to his promise of "I'll be back!" the Terminator had returned with a vengeance, and a new line: "*Hasta la vista*, baby."

In 1993, the release of *Last Action Hero* was greeted with enthusiasm by fans across America. However, the film opened to mixed reviews and did not perform as well as studio executives had hoped.

Still, Arnold forges ahead with a list of new films he's considering. There's the role of a marine turned tooth fairy in a comedy called *Sweet Tooth*. And there are film projects with his old colleagues Ivan Reitman and James Cameron, the man who directed *Terminator*.

Above all, Arnold is determined to bring his own distinctive mark to each film—that clever combination of iron man and funny guy. "I think that my mixture has been really good," said Arnold. "The people want two things from me. They want me to be tough and take care of the job and do it in a heroic way. And at the

Arnold and Austin O'Brian, his sidekick in Last Action Hero

same time, they want me to be funny and humorous. So
I give them both."

No matter what film Arnold decides to star in, one
thing is indisputable.

He'll be back.

6

Winning Over the World

When *Twins* opened in 1988, one of the guests at the premiere was President-elect George Bush, who claimed that he "was sure grateful" to Arnold during the last campaign. Arnold had donated money and support to the Bush campaign. His campaign speeches had won over voters in many states. Some Republicans commented that it was Arnold who won the state of Ohio for Bush!

Two years later, President Bush selected Arnold Schwarzenegger as chairman of the President's Council on Physical Fitness and Sports. It was a position that Arnold pursued with the same dedication that had made him a winning bodybuilder and star. Soon he was appearing on television shows and videos, encouraging kids to get the exercise they needed to stay healthy. Arnold was determined to get the word out—it was time for America to get fit!

Arnold helps out former President George Bush as head of the President's Council on Physical Fitness and Sports.

Arnold works out with a group of young fans.

Arnold's can-do attitude spills over into his personal life. These days, as a film star, husband, and father of three, he's got to change a few diapers as well as meet the demands of appearing on film. But Arnold takes it all in stride. Caring for his children is one more thing to master, and he has a winning attitude.

"We all have a great inner power," he said. "The power is self-faith. There's really an attitude to winning.

You have to see yourself winning before you win. And you have to be hungry. You have to want to conquer."

With his positive attitude, Arnold Schwarzenegger won a record-breaking seven Mr. Olympia titles. And with his distinctive combination of macho charisma and humor, Arnold has become a film hero capable of winning over the world.

Index

About the Author

Jack North is a writer who lives in New York City. A former minor league baseball player, he now spends his time covering film, celebrities, and sports events. From April to September, he can be found in Yankee stadium cheering on the Bronx Bombers.